Helping Children See Jesus

ISBN: 978-1-64104-022-8

The Providence of God
Old Testament Volume 8:
Exodus Part 3

Author: Arlene Piepgrass
Illustrator: Vernon Henkel
Computer Graphic Artist: Joshua Day
Typesetting and Layout: Morgan Melton, Patricia Pope

© 2018 Bible Visuals International
PO Box 153, Akron, PA 17501-0153
Phone: (717) 859-1131
www.biblevisuals.org

All rights reserved. No part of this publication may be reproduced, stored in a retrieval system or transmitted in any form by any means, electronic, mechanical, photocopy, recording or otherwise, without the prior permission of the publisher, except as provided by USA copyright law.

RELATED ITEMS

To access related items (such as activities, memory verse posters and translated texts) please visit our web store at shop.biblevisuals.org and enter 2008 in the search box on the page.

FREE TEXT DOWNLOAD

To access a FREE printable copy of the teaching text (PDF format) in English or other available languages, enter S2008DL in the search box. Add the item to your cart, and use coupon code XTACSV17 at checkout. Once your order is processed you will receive an email with a link to the free download.

It is good for me that I have been afflicted; that I might learn Thy statutes.

Psalm 119:71

Lesson 1
GOD PROVIDES WATER

Scripture to be studied: Exodus 15:1-27; 17:1-7

The *aim* of the lesson: To show that God knows the needs of His people and is able to provide for them.

What your students should *know*: Because God works according to His purpose, He may not provide everything immediately.

What your students should *feel*: An assurance of God's love and care when they are in need.

What your students should *do*: Tell God about their needs and trust Him to provide according to His will.

Lesson outline (for the teacher's and students' notebooks):
1. People need water (Exodus 15:22-23).
2. Although the people complain, God provides water (Exodus 15:24-25).
3. The people ignore the power of God (Exodus 17:1-3).
4. The people need the help of God (Exodus 17:1-7).

The verse to be memorized:

It is good for me that I have been afflicted; that I might learn Thy statutes. (Psalm 119:71)

NOTE TO THE TEACHER

Divine providence is God's continuous care over everything He created. His care includes a personal concern for each of His people. He knows all about us; even the hairs of our head are numbered (Matthew 10:30). He sees us (Psalm 33:13). He knows our needs (Matthew 6:32). He has the power to meet our needs (Philippians 4:19). He loves us (John 3:16). In all things God works for our spiritual good.

We must *not* blame the providence of God for the bad things we suffer. God did not create evil. Difficulties and suffering are the result of man's sinful disobedience. Only because of God's providence is there any good in the world.

Throughout the lesson, refer to the map on the back cover.

We are bringing together the two events of God's providing water as recorded in Exodus 16 and 17. Actually these were separated by the time spent in Elim and in the wilderness of Sin where God provided meat and manna, as taught in Exodus 16.

THE LESSON

Did you ever go on a long hike when the sun was hot? Did you take water with you? What happened when the water was all gone? (Let the students discuss.)

1. PEOPLE NEED WATER
Exodus 15:22-23

Next to the air we breathe, water is the most important thing in life. The normal person may live for weeks without food. But he can live only a few days without water. God knows our need for water. He created us this way.

The Israelites, having left Egypt, turned their backs to the Red Sea. By His power, God had led them safely through the sea. They were amazed and talked happily. "We are free! FREE! No slave masters to shout at us or beat us. No soldiers to frighten us! We are going to our homeland. We are free!"

Suddenly the cloud of God began to move. "Look! The cloud is moving southward!" "Pick up your belongings." "We're on our way!" Everyone shouted at once.

Moses and Aaron walked ahead of the great crowd. Could they have said something like this?

Moses began, "Pharaoh tried to destroy our people. He thought he could defeat us. Instead, God multiplied our numbers. Now, here we are, more than two million people!"

Aaron asked, "How do you suppose we will ever have enough food and water for everyone? It will take many days to get to Canaan."

"I wish I could answer that question, Aaron," Moses replied. "I lived in this wilderness for 40 years. There really is little here to eat or drink. But God knows what He's doing. We must trust Him. He will meet our needs somehow. I wonder why the cloud of God is directing us south. It would be much closer to go up along the north coast (Point out on map.)

All day long they walked under the hot sun. Happy, because they were free, they sang praises to God.

Show Illustration #1

After the people set up camp for the night, some men came to Moses. "Moses, our children are thirsty. Our water bags are almost empty. Where can we get water?" (*Teacher:* Explain that people carried water in bags made of goat skins.)

Moses answered confidently, "God knows we need water. He will provide. Rest now. Trust Him."

Like the Israelites, we too need certain things. God wants us to believe He is able to supply them.

2. ALTHOUGH THE PEOPLE COMPLAIN, GOD PROVIDES WATER
Exodus 15:24-25

The morning dawned and again the cloud moved.

Little children everywhere were crying. "I'm thirsty!" Mothers tried to comfort them. "Moses said God will help us find water."

The sun grew hotter. The women and children grew weary. The water bags were empty. Everyone was thirsty. "When are we going to find the water Moses promised?" they asked one another.

No one was praising God for having opened the Red Sea. No one remembered how their Egyptian enemies were drowned in the Sea. No one was thanking God for their freedom from slavery.

All day long they grumbled impatiently. "We're thirsty!"

Unhappiness spread through the camp that night. "It's easy for Moses to say God will provide. But we're people, not angels. We need water to drink."

Complaining is catching. As the third day began, no one was happy.

Moses asked, "Have you forgotten how God led you out of Egypt only three days ago? Remember how He killed the first born son in each Egyptian home? He spared our sons, you know. We belong to Him. And He will soon lead us to water."

But no one would listen. They did not think about God. They thought only of finding water. Finally their complaining turned to silence. Wearily they plodded along pitying themselves.

Suddenly the silence was broken. "Look! There's water ahead!"

The strongest raced to the springs. Stooping, they cupped their hands and drank deeply.

"Ugh!" they cried, spitting out the water. "We can't drink this. It is bitter. It will make us sick!" And two million people wailed desperately.

Angrily, they turned to Moses. "What are we going to do?" they shouted. "What are we supposed to drink? Don't tell us God will mysteriously supply. We want action!"

Moses could have scolded the people. He might have said, "I am going to quit being your leader. I am tired of your grumbling and complaining. Find water yourself."

Instead, Moses prayed, "O God, You have led us out of Egypt. You brought us through the Red Sea by your mighty power. You know we are thirsty. You know we must have water to drink. Please show me what to do for all these people."

God answered, "Moses, cut down that tree over there. Throw it into the water."

Quickly Moses obeyed. Turning to the people, he commanded, "Drink the water now!"

Show Illustration #2

A few sipped it. "It's good!" they shouted. "It's pure! We can drink all we need! God really is faithful. He has provided for us. We shall never doubt Him again. We shall never again complain."

Listen to the people around you. Listen to yourself. Do you complain rather than talk to God about your needs? Do you act as if God doesn't care or can't provide for you? Do you (like the Israelites) forget what He did for you yesterday or last week? Do you live thankfully telling God you know He'll take care of you as He promised? If we aren't thankful in everything, God is displeased. (See 1 Thessalonians 5:18.)

3. THE PEOPLE IGNORE THE POWER OF GOD
Exodus 17:1-3

Days stretched into weeks as the Israelites traveled south in the wilderness. When they came to Rephidim, they were again thirsty. They searched for water in the cracks of the rocks. The children were crying. The sheep were bleating. The cattle were lowing. Everyone wanted water.

What do you suppose the mothers and fathers did this time? (Let students discuss.) Surely they would think of God's power. They would remember how He provided the water they needed at Marah. They would wait patiently for God to supply again. Certainly they would trust Him.

Show Illustration #3

But listen to what they said to Moses. "Why did you bring us out of Egypt? Are you trying to kill with thirst? Are you trying to kill our children and all our animals? We want water and we want it NOW!"

"Why are you angry with me?" Moses asked. "Why are you doubting God? He alone has power to supply water."

Refusing to listen, the angry mob shouted, "We don't even believe the Lord is here with us! If He were, we could find water to drink! He has forgotten all about us."

Moses cried, "O God, what will I do with these people? They are ready to kill me!"

4. THE PEOPLE NEED THE HELP OF GOD
Exodus 17:1-7

The people needed the help of God alone. Moses could not help them. There was no water in sight. They deserved God's anger and punishment. Instead, lovingly and patiently, God spoke to Moses. "Do not be discouraged, Moses. I am with you. Choose some of the leaders. Take your rod and go to the rock on Mount Horeb, " God commanded. "Strike the rock with your rod. I will send from it enough water for all the people and animals."

"Water out of a rock? How is this possible? Suppose I strike it and nothing happens. What then?" Moses *could* have asked such questions.

Show Illustration #4

Instead, he believed God. So he did exactly what God commanded. He struck the rock. And a miraculous flow of water gushed out. There was plenty for all.

Suppose God had shown Moses beforehand how He was going to supply the needs of this great army of people. Would it have made things easier for Moses? Would it have been better for the people if their needs had been met without having to wait? (Allow discussion.)

God wanted His people to know that He can provide every need. He wanted them to depend on Him alone for everything. He wanted to teach them that He is faithful.

Do you ever say to yourself, "I do not believe God cares about me. If He did, He would not let me suffer. He would not make me wait. He would answer all my prayers immediately."

Our memory verse reminds us that sometimes we must have difficulties so we can learn God's laws. God wants us to obey Him and depend upon Him. He wants us to cast all our cares on Him (1 Peter 5:7). He wants us to believe Him even when He does not give us everything we ask for.

Believing God, even in times of trouble, is sure to give us peace, joy and contentment. Do you need something today? Write it in your notebook. Then we shall tell God about this need. Together we will trust Him. If it is His perfect will for you to have it, He will supply it in His time.

Lesson 2
GOD PROVIDES FOOD

Scripture to be studied: Exodus 16; Psalm 78

The *aim* of the lesson: To show the necessity of depending entirely upon God.

What your students should *know*: Complaining comes when they do not trust God.

What your students should *feel*: A hatred for murmuring and complaining.

What your students should *do*: Deal with the sin of complaining.

Lesson outline (for the teacher's and students' notebooks):

1. The people do not trust God (Exodus 16:1-3).
2. God proves He is all sufficient (Exodus 16:4, 6-18).
3. God tests His people (Exodus 16:4-5; 23-26).
4. The people disobey God (Exodus 16:20-28).

The verse to be memorized:

It is good for me that I have been afflicted; that I might learn Thy statutes. (Psalm 119:71)

NOTE TO THE TEACHER

The providence of God is His care and supervision of all creation. Providence is God–the all-powerful, all-knowing One–doing what He purposes for all of creation, including mankind.

In the study of providence, we observe two truths: (1) God is in absolute control of everything. (2) Yet God allows people the freedom to make choices. These two facts are clear in this lesson.

In tracing on the map the wanderings of God's people you will see that they went from Marah (where water was first provided, Exodus 15:23-25) to Elim (Exodus 15:27); from Elim to the Wilderness of Sin to Rephidim (Exodus 17:1); and from Rephidim to Mount Horeb (where God again provided water, Exodus 17:5-7). This may be confusing to your people, because of our having combined the two accounts of the provision of water (See Lesson #1, Exodus 15 and 17.). In this lesson we go back to Exodus 16. Please make it clear that the people did not hop back and forth.

THE LESSON

While God's people (the Israelites) lived in Egypt, God caused them to be ruled over by Pharaoh, the king. Pharaoh told them where could live, what they could do, and where they could go. They were forced to work for him and obey what he said. Any Israelite who disobeyed, was lashed. Pharaoh, like Satan, did not care about giving the people what was best for them.

When the Israelites left Egypt, God chose Moses to speak to the people for Him. God himself guided them. He led them in the pillar of cloud by day, and the pillar of fire by night. By looking at the cloud or fire, they could see that God was with them. When the cloud moved, they moved. When the cloud stopped, they pitched their tents and rested.

The people should have believed that God would take care of them. He had promised He would. (See Exodus 13:5.) But they did not believe Him.

1. THE PEOPLE DO NOT TRUST GOD
Exodus 16:1-3

People today are like those Israelites. They don't trust God.

God caused the people to camp for a time at Elim. There was plenty of water there and palm trees for shade. (See Exodus 15:27.) Now it was time to move on. Following the cloud of God, they moved into a deserted place called the Wilderness of Sin. (*Teacher:* Indicate on map.)

Show Illustration #5

"Where will we find food here?" many asked. "There are no farms, no towns, no markets. There is no one from whom to buy anything."

On and on they walked through the wilderness day after day. At first, only a small group complained. Soon the discontent spread. People were hungry. Unhappy people always blame someone for their troubles.

"Where are Moses and Aaron leading us? How do they expect to feed us out here?" Everyone grumbled–fathers, mothers, children. "If only we had stayed in Egypt! At least we had plenty of food there!"

What had they forgotten about Egypt? (*Teacher:* Discuss, allowing the students to recall the slavery, murder of babies, impossible work required, lashings by slavemasters.)

"Moses led us out here to kill us with hunger," wept the mothers. "We've been tricked."

Moses and Aaron tried to quiet the people. "Do not blame us. We didn't bring you here. God did. You really don't believe God can take care of you, do you? Look ahead. God is with us. See the cloud? He didn't lead us out of Egypt to kill us. He knows we need food. He will supply for us. Remember! He gave us water when we needed it. Things are really good here in the wilderness. We are FREE! We can worship God. We can enjoy our families. God is taking us to our homeland!" Moses said cheerfully.

But the people did not thank God for His goodness. They did not ask Him to supply their need. Instead, they murmured more and more. "Can God furnish a table in the wilderness?" they asked. (See Psalm 78:19.)

When we have problems, it is just as easy for us to forget all God's blessings. We are tempted to say, "God has forgotten me. He is going to let me die."

2. GOD PROVES HE IS ALL-SUFFICIENT
Exodus 16:4, 6-18

God knew they needed food. He knew they couldn't find anything to eat in the wilderness. He told Moses, "I'm going to rain down bread from Heaven! They belong to Me. They must trust Me!"

How good God is! He should have been angry with His people. They should have been punished for their unbelief. Instead, God pitied them and forgave them. (See Psalm 78:38-39.)

God is exactly as kind to us today. He does not give us the punishment we deserve for our sins: death. He offers us forgiveness of sin and eternal life through His Son.

Moses and Aaron gathered the people together to speak to them. "God has heard your grumbling. Now He will show you He is powerful enough to supply all you need. In the evening He will send quails (birds) so you can have meat to eat. In the morning He is going to rain bread from Heaven. You will be able to eat until you are filled. And you will know that He is Lord your God!"

"How can God send enough bread for all of us?" the grumblers asked. "Who ever heard of bread being sent from Heaven? It is impossible! The only way to get bread is to plant grain and wait for it to grow."

They had failed to understand that with God NOTHING is impossible! (See Jeremiah 32:17; Luke 1:37.) Like us, they tried to think of a way God could meet their needs. But God's ways are much better than our ways! (See Isaiah 55:8-9.)

Show Illustration #6

That evening, exactly as He had promised, God sent flocks of quails. All 2 million people had meat. No one went to bed hungry that night! (See Psalm 78:29.)

3. GOD TESTS HIS PEOPLE
Exodus 16:4-5, 23-26

The next morning, the ground was covered with fine white flakes–something they had never seen before.

"What is this? What do we do with it?" the people asked.

Moses answered, "This is manna. It's the bread God has given us to eat. Listen carefully. He has told us exactly how to gather the manna and use it. We are to get up early in the morning and go out to collect it. When the sun gets hot, it will melt and disappear.

"You must gather an omer (quart and a half measure) for each one in your family. That is how much the Lord will provide."

(Since there were at least 2 million people, 3 million quarts of manna were needed every day. How great is God's power!)

Moses continued, "God has commanded that you gather a fresh supply every morning. Do not try to store it overnight. Do you understand?"

Show Illustration #7

"Yes, yes, we understand," the people replied. Eagerly they picked up their shares.

Once again songs of praise to God could be heard throughout the camp.

When they ate the manna they exclaimed . "It is delicious! This is better than the bread we had in Egypt. God is good to us."

These for whom God provided so well would surely not forget His instructions! Certainly they would obey Him and trust Him now! But listen!

4. THE PEOPLE DISOBEY GOD
Exodus 16:20-28

A mother said, "I am going to save some manna for tomorrow. Then if there should be none to gather in the morning, we shall still have plenty to eat." Others liked her idea.

Their husbands agreed "Very good! We won't have to get up as early in the morning. We can simply eat what is left over."

But what had God commanded? (*Teacher:* Encourage student response.) These people were disobeying God.

Show Illustration #8

The next morning from each of these tents there was an awful smell. When they went to eat the manna they wailed, "It's full of worms!" How ashamed they were!

They had not believed that God would do what He promised. They had disobeyed Him.

On the sixth morning, Moses had an announcement. "God has commanded that we gather twice as much manna today. Tomorrow is the day of rest. He will not send any manna tomorrow. Use half that you collect today. Save the rest for tomorrow."

"It will be full of worms if we keep it overnight," some insisted.

Moses replied, "No, what you keep will still be fresh in the morning."

The next day when Moses looked out his tent, what do you think he saw? Men and women had their pans and were looking for manna! Did they find any? No! God meant what He said. But they had not believed Him. Nor had they followed His directions.

God saw His rebellious people, too. Sadly He said to Moses, "How long will these people refuse to obey Me?"

As God looks down on you today, what does He see? Does He see that you trust Him? Does He see you are depending upon Him for everything? Does He hear your lips thanking Him for good and perfect gifts? (See James 1:17.) Does He see that you are thankful even for difficult circumstances? (*Teacher:* Review the memory verse.)

Or does God hear lips that are grumbling and complaining? Does He see someone who is worrying? He tells us not to worry about anything. Rather we are to tell Him about our needs and thank Him for Hosanswers. (See Philippians 4:6.)

List in your notebook anything you are doing that displeases God. Mention also what you can do to correct these things this week. Together we shall pray that, always in everything, you will trust God completely. We shall pray, too, that your life will constantly be filled with praise–even in hard places.

The greatest provision which God has made for us is salvation through His Son, Jesus Christ. We deserve eternal punishment in hell because of our sin. But God offers us eternal life if we will trust Christ. He says "He that believeth on the Son hath everlasting life and he that believeth not the Son shall not see life but the wrath of God abideth on him" (John 3:36). Will you place your trust in Him today?

Lesson 3
GOD PROVIDES PROTECTION

Scripture to be studied: Exodus 17:8-16; all verses in lesson

The *aim* of the lesson: To show that God's enemy, Satan, is always attacking God's people.

What your students should *know*: That God is more powerful than Satan and provides protection against him.

What your students should *feel*: The uselessness of fighting Satan in their own strength.

What your students should *do*: Draw near to God; resist the devil until he flees from them (See James 4:7-8.).

Lesson outline (for the teacher's and students' notebooks):
1. The nature of the enemy (Genesis 25:27-34; Deuteronomy 25:18).
2. The attack of the enemy (Exodus 17:8; Deuteronomy 25:17-18).
3. The protection of God (Exodus 17:9-10).
4. The victory through prayer (Exodus 17:11-16).

The verse to be memorized:

It is good for me that I have been afflicted; that I might learn Thy statutes. (Psalm 119:71)

NOTE TO THE TEACHER

Since creation, Satan has attempted to overthrow God's program. He persuaded Adam and Eve to disobey God. He tried to destroy God's nation, Israel. He attempted to get rid of the Lord Jesus shortly after His birth. He blinded men's eyes so they rejected Christ and crucified Him. The devil is still trying to destroy the program of God.

Satan is our enemy today. He is like a roaring lion, trying to destroy us (1 Peter 5:8). But God is greater than Satan (1 John 4:4). And, as we trust Him to do so, He gives us the power to resist the devil (See 1 Peter 5:8; James 4:7-8.).

THE LESSON

Do you think it was easy for Moses to lead two million Israelites? Who chose Moses? God knew it would be hard. That is why He had arranged for Moses to be carefully trained. (1) God gave Moses parents who prayed for him and taught him about the true God. (2) In the palace in Egypt, God arranged for Moses to learn how to lead people. (3) Then, when Moses was 40 years old, God sent him to the wilderness. There for 40 years he learned how to live a rugged life. He learned to trust God in places of danger.

God knew all the difficulties His people would have in the wilderness. So He trained Moses to be the kind of leader they needed.

Moses was "mighty in words and in deeds" (Acts 7:22) during the years he was in Pharaoh's palace. From a history book we learn that Moses was a great soldier. When the Ethiopians invaded Egypt, Moses commanded the Egyptian army and defeated the enemy.

Now, Moses was commander-in-chief of another army, the Israelites.

God was teaching the Israelites to depend on Him alone. When they were thirsty, He gave them water. When they were hungry, He supplied food. Now they were going to learn what it meant to have enemies. Could God protect them and give them victory?

1. THE NATURE OF THE ENEMY
Genesis 25:27-34; Deuteronomy 25:18

The people of God were not alone in the wilderness. God was not the only One who was watching what they were doing. The wilderness was the home of wandering tribespeople. They went from place to place trying to find water and pasture for their animals.

Show Illustration #9

These tribes were watching the Israelites. They knew where the Israelites were at all times. They weren't happy to have these uninvited "invaders" in their land.

These people, the Amalekites, were the most powerful of all the desert tribes. They were wild, fierce and warlike. But who were they? Where did they come from?

More than 500 years before this, twin boys, Jacob and Esau, were born. Esau was firstborn and should have had the blessing which each Jewish father gave to his oldest son. But Jacob, by lying, had cheated Esau out of his blessing. Because of this Esau threatened to kill Jacob. So Jacob had to run for his life.

In time, both Jacob and Esau married and had children, grandchildren, greatgrandchildren. The Israelites were the descendants of Jacob. They served Jehovah, the living God. The Amalekites were the descendants of Esau. They did not worship God. (See Deuteronomy 25:18.) They hated the descendants of Jacob because of what had happened long before. So they became helpers of Satan, God's enemy, who wanted to destroy the people of God.

2. THE ATTACK OF THE ENEMY
Exodus 17:8; Deuteronomy 25:17-18

Show Illustration #10

The Amalekite chiefs met together to discuss what should be done about this army of strangers. They may have said something like this:

"These slaves from Egypt should have gone up the north coast on their way to Canaan." (indicate route on map.) "Now they've come south. They're using our pasture for their animals. If we don't stop them, they will take over our whole country. Let's attack them!"

"Wait a minute," another leader insisted. "I've been told that God opened up the Red Sea. And that whole crowd of Israelites walked through on dry ground! The Egyptians (who were trying to catch the Israelites) were swallowed by the sea."

"Not only that," added another. "God has been covering the ground around them every morning with strange-looking

– 23 –

flakes. I hear they gather them and use them to make bread. Just this week their leader struck a rock. Ever since water has been flowing from it. Somebody or something must be taking care of them."

The first leader spoke proudly. "No one is too strong for us. Remember, these people are slaves. They don't know how to fight. They've never gone to war. They probably don't even know how to hold a sword! All they do is grumble and complain. It should be easy to defeat them. Those who are lagging behind are old or tired. (See Deuteronomy 25:17-18.) So we shall attack them first. Then our soldiers will descend on the whole camp and take them captive. We'll make them our servants." Proudly the Amalekites made their plans.

3. THE PROTECTION OF GOD
Exodus 17:9-10

God heard their wicked plans. He watched their soldiers sharpen their swords and spears.

God saw how frightened His people were. "We are not trained to fight," they cried. These Amalekites are fierce and powerful. We are nothing!" They were too afraid now to grumble and complain!

"God told Moses what to do when we needed food and water," one comforted another. "I hope He will tell Moses what to do now!"

Moses was not afraid. He could see the rock where God had stood with him. He could hear the gurgling of the water as it flowed from that rock. He knew God could protect them.

He remembered how God had defeated Pharaoh and his powerful Egyptian army. Moses knew that God was mightier than any army on earth.

Show Illustration #11

Turning to a young man, Moses commanded, "Joshua, choose an army of strong men to fight against the Amalekites tomorrow. I shall take my rod and go to the top of that hill. You will be able to see me. There I shall pray to God for victory,"

4. THE VICTORY THROUGH PRAYER
Exodus 17:11-16

As Joshua led his soldiers out to battle the next morning, they saw Moses on the hilltop. His rod was in his hand. Both arms were lifted toward Heaven.

Show Illustration #12

"Come on, men!" Joshua shouted. "Moses is praying for us! God will hear! He will fight for us! Charge!"

To the surprise of the Amalekites, these Israelites were strong. They knew how to fight. Israel was winning!

Joshua's men began to grow weary. The Amalekites were gaining and the Israelites were being pushed back. Looking up, Joshua saw that Moses' hands had dropped to his sides.

"Moses! Moses!" Joshua shouted. "Raise your rod! Pray to God!"

As Moses lifted his hands, the Israelites were reminded of God's presence. They remembered His great power. And they pushed forward with fresh strength. The Amalekites were shoved back.

The sun rose high in the sky and the battle continued. Moses became so weary he could no longer hold up his hands. But when he lowered them, Israel was overrun.

"Moses, come sit on this stone," his brother suggested. "Hur and I will hold up your arms for you."

Moses' arms were held high until the sun went down. And the enemy was defeated for the Lord God of Israel is all-powerful.

God told Moses, "Write the events of this day in a book. I do not want the people ever to forget what happened today. I want you to talk about it over and over. I want your descendants to know how I protected you. Remember, I am the One who gave you victory over your enemy today."

Moses did not build a statue of Joshua to honor him. No! He built an altar to God. He named it, "The Lord is my banner," because the Lord God had won the victory.

If your trust is in God's Son, you are a child of God. His great enemy, Satan, will attack you. He will tempt you to lie, to cheat, to steal. He will try to make you do all sorts of sinful things.

Sometimes, as an angel of light (2 Corinthians 11:14), he makes sinful things look good. The Bible calls Stan "a roaring lion" (See 1 Peter 5:8.). But God is stronger than Satan. And He is able to defeat him when he attacks you. (See 1 John 4:4.)

God tells us to draw near to Him. He says "Resist the devil and he will flee from you." (See James 4:7-8.)

In what ways is Satan attacking you this day? Please list these in your notebooks. If you've taken something that does not belong to you, will you promise God right now that you'll return it to the owner? If you've told someone a lie, will you correct it today? (*Teacher:* Name other sins with which your students may be attacked.) The only way we can resist the devil is by studying God's Word and praying to Him. Will you promise Him now that you'll read His Word and pray each day?

If you don't belong to God's family, will you turn to the Lord Jesus right now? He is the Son of God. Do you believe this? If so, ask Him to forgive your sins. Thank Him for dying for you. Thank Him that He proved He is the Son of God by rising from the dead. Will you place all your trust in Him this moment?

Lesson 4
GOD PROVIDES FOR US TODAY

NOTE TO THE TEACHER

God is sovereign. That is, He is Creator of all things–things we can see; things we cannot see. He owns everything. He has, therefore, the absolute right to rule over all. (See Matthew 20:15; Romans 9:20-21.) And He does. (See Ephesians 1:11.)

This sovereign control is called Providence. Providence refers to the continuous activity of God by which He makes everything work out His purposes. Even the evil that has entered the universe does not hinder His wise and holy purpose.

God exercises sovereign rule over all the physical universe (Psalm 103:19; Job 9:5-7, 38:12-35; Matthew 5:46), over animal creation (Job 12:10; Psalm 104:21, 28-29; Matthew 10:29), over the nations of the earth (Job 12:23; Psalm 22:28; Romans 13:1), and over all individuals (Jeremiah 1:5; Galatians 1:15-16).

By His providence, God is over each person's birth, his successes and failures (See Psalm 75:6-7). He is over the seemingly insignificant things in life (Matthew 10:30). He is over the needs of His people (Romans 8:28; Philippians 4:19), which is the subject of our study in this volume.

Scripture to be studied: 1 Corinthians 10:1-13; John 6:1-58; 17:1-26

The *aim* of the lesson: To show that God has lessons for us from the things which happened to people in Bible times.

What your students should *know*: Although God provides many of our needs for this life, He is even more concerned about our spiritual needs.

What your students should *feel*: A desire to turn from sin and live according to the Word of God.

What your students should *do*:
Unsaved: Place their trust in the Saviour.
Saved: Deal immediately with any sin that is in their lives.

Lesson outline for the teacher's and students' notebooks:
1. Jesus: the smitten Rock (1 Corinthians 10:1-6).
2. Jesus: the Bread of Life (John 6:1-58).
3. Jesus prays for us (John 17:1-26).
4. Examples and warnings for us (1 Corinthians 10:1-13).

The verse to be memorized:

It is good for me that I have been afflicted; that I might learn Thy statutes. (Psalm 119:71)

THE LESSON

Why do you suppose God kept a record in His Word of the things which happened to the Israelites? Those events took place more than 3,000 year ago. Why should we study them now? (*Teacher:* Encourage group discussion.)

God Himself answers those questions. His Word says, "... All these things happened to them to show us the way God works. They were written as examples and warnings for us." (See 1 Corinthians 10:11.)

Thinking of our last three lessons, let us talk about the experiences God's people had in the wilderness. They did and said many things. *What have you learned about yourself from them?* (*Teacher:* Refer to specific examples: their unbelief; fear; grumbling; their great need for food and water.) Are you ever like the Israelites?

Think of what God for the Israelites in the wilderness. *What have you learned about God?* (*Teacher:* Encourage student response. Remember: His omnipotence–He has all power; His omniscience–He knows everything, so He knew their needs; His faithfulness; His patience; His love; His guidance–the pillars of cloud and fire.)

1. JESUS: THE SMITTEN ROCK
1 Corinthians 10:1-6

When the Israelites were wandering in the wilderness, they needed water. Oh, how they needed water! All two million of them! But there was no water anywhere. Moses, their leader, knew of no way to get water for them–except to ask God for it. And that is what he did. God, who knows all things, knew they were thirsty. Because He loved His people, He wanted them to have all they needed. So He came to their rescue.

Show Illustration #13

God commanded, "Moses, strike the rock with your rod." Moses obeyed. And streams of water gushed from the rock. The people drank; the animals drank. There was enough for all.

Because God provided water for His thirsty people long ago, we know He can provide for us too. But from this particular event, God wants us to know another truth. Many, many years later He recorded in His Word, "That Rock was Christ" (1 Corinthians 10:4). He was so eager for His people to know what His Son would be like, He gave them word pictures of Him before He came.

Moses struck the rock. And the Lord Christ was smitten (See Isaiah 53:5-6.). The soldiers who nailed Him to the cross pierced His side with a sword. Speaking of this beforehand, Jesus said, "This is My blood . . . which is shed for many for the forgiveness of sins." For this reason the Lord Jesus had come to earth. We are sinful–all of us. We cannot help ourselves. Because God cannot overlook evil, our sins must be punished. The Lord Jesus never sinned. Yet He took all our sins on Himself and died in our place. (See 1 Peter 2:22-24.)

Have you ever struck a rock with a stick? Did it destroy the rock? No. Just so, death did not destroy the Rock, Christ Jesus. He "tasted death" for everyone. (See Hebrews 2:9.) But He, God the Son, did not–could not–stay dead. He arose and is alive forevermore.

What did the Israelites have to do to have their thirst satisfied? They had to drink the water. Just so, those who want to have their sins forgiven, must place their trust in Jesus Christ, God's Son. He died for all. But only those who believe in Him can have forgiveness of sin. Only by receiving Him can they have life eternal (See John 4:14.).

Are you trusting in the Rock, Christ Jesus?

2. JESUS, THE BREAD OF LIFE
John 6:1-58

While the Lord Jesus was here on earth, many listened to His good preaching. Once, a Jewish boy grabbed his lunch and went with the crowd which was following Jesus. Setting his lunch down alongside him, he listened to Jesus. He was so interested, he forgot about being hungry. Then he heard the Lord Jesus and His disciples talking about feeding everyone.

One of the disciples, Philip, said, "Even if there was a place to buy bread, we do not have enough money."

Another disciple, Andrew, said, "Lord, there is a boy here. He has five biscuits and two small fish. But that is nothing for such a crowd!"

Jesus answered, "Bring them to Me. And tell the people to sit down." Quietly He looked up toward Heaven and thanked God for the food.

Show Illustration #14

The boy's eyes grew big with amazement as he watched Jesus breaking his bread and dividing his fish. Jesus kept breaking and breaking and breaking. The food just never ended. Everyone in that huge crowd (there were 5,000 men–besides women and children!) ate until they were filled!

"Gather up the left-overs." Jesus told His disciples. "Do not waste anything."

Imagine the boy's surprise when he saw 12 baskets of left-overs!

On the way home, the people came to a decision. "Let's make this man our king. He will be able to feed us and we shall not have to work anymore."

The next day they found Jesus. And they were surprised when they discovered He knew their thoughts of the day before. He told them, "You seek Me only because I fed you with bread and fish. Now you are hungry again. Do not think only about the food that comes and goes. Look for the spiritual food–everlasting life–which the Son of Man can give you . . . It is the will of God that you believe in Me–the One He has sent." (See John 6:27-29.)

"How do we know You came from God?" the crowd demanded. "In the wild desert, our fathers ate manna which Moses gave them. That was a greater miracle than your feeding the people yesterday."

The Lord Jesus answered, "It was My Father, God–not Moses–who sent the manna to feed the Israelites. They ate it and were hungry again the next day. They ate that bread and died. But I am the Bread of Life. I have come down from Heaven. If anyone trusts in Me, he will never hunger again."

The crowd didn't understand.

Jesus explained, "Do you want to live forever? Do you want to have eternal life? Trust Me. I am the living Bread. When you believe in Me, you receive My life–everlasting life. You will be forever with God and Me in Heaven. This is far more important than simply living here on earth."

Have you placed *your* trust in Jesus, God the Son?

3. JESUS PRAYS FOR US
John 17:1-26

When God's people, the Israelites, fought against their enemy, the Amalekites, the battle went well for a while. Why? (*Teacher:* Show Illustration #12 and encourage discussion.) When Moses prayed to God for the Israelites, they were able to defeat the enemy.

We have an enemy today. What is his name? (Satan, the devil.) We need someone to pray to God for us. God has provided that Person. The Lord Jesus Christ who lives forever, prays for us. (See Isaiah 53:12; 1 John 2:1; Romans 8:27; Hebrews 7:25.) Because He prays all the time, our enemy, Satan can be defeated.

Show Illustration #15

Even before He went to Heaven, Jesus prayed to God, asking:

1. That God would keep us from doing the sinful things of this world (See John 17:15. Do you see the two fighting each other?).
2. That we would live clean, pure lives according to God's Word (See John 17:17. Do you read the Bible every day?).
3. That we would love others so much, that many will turn to the Lord Christ (See John 17:21,23.).
4. That we shall live with Him forever when life on earth is over (See John 17:24. The cloud at the top of the illustration reminds us of Heaven.).

The Lord Jesus Christ wants us to have a wonderful life here on earth. He has done and is doing all He can to make it so. Are you letting Him have His way? Or do you give in to Satan?

4. EXAMPLES AND WARNINGS FOR US
1 Corinthians 10:1-13

The things which happened in the long ago were written in the Bible as examples for us. From their experiences we know what God approves of and what He hates.

Perhaps you are thinking, *I am not like the Israelites. I do not grumble. I am not ungrateful. I would not criticize others–as they criticized Moses and Aaron.*

But listen! God says, ". . . the person who thinks he can stand against sin had better watch that he does not fall into sin." (See 1 Corinthians 10:12.) Maybe you will not sin exactly the same as the Israelites did. If you have enough food and water, you do not crave that. But maybe you crave other things: clothes, candy, gum. (*Teacher:* Name things your students want.) And, if you don't get them, you grumble and complain.

Or do you gossip and repeat things about others that may not be true? God hates this.

Maybe you do not bow down to gods of wood and stone. You know such idols are worthless nothings. But maybe popularity is your idol. You want people to know who you are. Perhaps you always want your own way. Always, wherever you are, you say to yourself, *ME FIRST.* If any of these are true of you, you have made an idol of yourself. And God hates this.

Show Illustration #16

Do you have wrong thoughts? Wrong desires? God knows all about our temptations (See 1 Corinthians 10:13.). None of the things that tempt us are too strong for Him. When evil thoughts come into your mind, pray to Him at once. Ask Him to take them away. Think of the truths you have learned from His Word.

Memorizing God's Word is the best weapon against evil thoughts. (See Psalm 119:9, 11.) God knows about all the evil temptations we have. He has given us the Bible so we can learn from those who lived long ago. It is up to us to study His Word – and obey it. And remember! The Lord Jesus who died and rose again, is greater, far more powerful, than Satan. (See 1 John 4:4.)

List in your notebook the sins which are tempting you. If God has already shown you how to deal with these temptations, write it down. Or, if you need help, I shall be glad to talk with you, if you wish. Then we shall pray together that God will help you to live according to His Word.

www.ingramcontent.com/pod-product-compliance
Lightning Source LLC
Chambersburg PA
CBHW060806090426
42736CB00002B/176